HEAVENLY ANGEL LAY LAY

EXPLAINS THE

<u>BIBLICAL GROUNDS</u>

<u>FOR MARRIAGE,</u>

<u>SEPARATION,</u>

<u>AND DIVORCE</u>

PUBLISHING COMPANY

ISBN: 978-0-6151-7481-5

www.crossover-ministries-publishing.com

ABOUT THE AUTHOR

I was dedicated to Jesus Christ of Nazareth as an infant and accepted Him as my Lord and Savior around seven years old when a visiting youth group led me in prayer at the alter. During my Salvation Prayer I asked Jesus to use me in a special ministry. Something that very few other Christians would want to do. I saw all the people just sitting in the pews, the ushers, and the Sunday School teachers and realized any Christian could do that. I wanted something different. One day in church service there was a visiting minister at a church I was visiting as well. The Minister said, "Jesus is going to make you a 'Healer of a Heart'". Then he asked me if I knew what that meant. I said, "No." the minister said, "I don't either, but whatever it is, Jesus is going to use you in a powerful way.

Helping Rachael, Jesus showed me what a 'Healer of the Heart' is. During the course of me helping Rachael to the 'Promised Land', a real Heavenly Angel named Lay Lay and I were allowed one hour one day to talk about Spiritual and Family situations from the King James Version of the Word of God. These books are designed to answer a lot of Spiritual Questions not even your minister can answer or your Church Denomination. I know theology Doctors who can't tell you how people other than Noah and his family made it past the 'Great Flood', yet their names are listed in the King James Version of the Word of God right after the 'World Wide Flood'. These books explain that and much more. I have written these books to tell the whole truth about the Word of God no matter how difficult it may be for me or others. Yes, there are things I write in these books that I don't even like, but in all fairness and total honestly, I must say the WHOLE TRUTH. The title of this book is 100% real. HEAVENLY ANGEL LAY LAY explained to me the biblical aspects of a Marriage, Separation, Divorce and Foster Care as well.

ABOUT THE AUTHOR

I was dedicated to Jesus Christ of Nazareth as an infant and accepted Him as my Lord and Savior around seven years old when a visiting youth group led me in prayer at the alter. During my Salvation Prayer I asked Jesus to use me in a special ministry. Something that very few other Christians would want to do. I saw all the people just sitting in the pews, the ushers, and the Sunday School teachers and realized any Christian could do that. I wanted something different. One day in church service there was a visiting minister at a church I was visiting as well. The Minister said, "Jesus is going to make you a 'Healer of a Heart'". Then he asked me if I knew what that meant. I said, "No." the minister said, "I don't either, but whatever it is, Jesus is going to use you in a powerful way.

Helping Rachael, Jesus showed me what a 'Healer of the Heart' is. During the course of me helping Rachael to the 'Promised Land', a real Heavenly Angel named Lay Lay and I were allowed one hour one day to talk about Spiritual and Family situations from the King James Version of the Word of God. These books are designed to answer a lot of Spiritual Questions not even your minister can answer or your Church Denomination. I know theology Doctors who can't tell you how people other than Noah and his family made it past the 'Great Flood', yet their names are listed in the King James Version of the Word of God right after the 'World Wide Flood'. These books explain that and much more. I have written these books to tell the whole truth about the Word of God no matter how difficult it may be for me or others. Yes, there are things I write in these books that I don't even like, but in all fairness and total honestly, I must say the WHOLE TRUTH. The title of this book is 100% real. HEAVENLY ANGEL LAY LAY explained to me the biblical aspects of a Marriage, Separation, Divorce and Foster Care as well.

INTRODUCTION

The first section of this book is about Biblical Aspects of Marriage, Separation, Divorce, and Foster Care. The second section of this book contains the good and bad times of Abraham and Sarah, Abraham and Keturah, and Isaac and Rebekah as couples. All scriptures are taken from the King James Version of the Word of God. This book contains an excerpt from my book. MATTHEW'S WORD 'TWO':REAL WORD OF GOD BIBLE.

BOOKS WRITTEN BY WALTER BURCHETT, BA:

MATTHEW'S WORD 'TWO':REAL WORD OF GOD BIBLE   ISBN: 1-4116-6995-9

HEAVENLY ANGEL LAY LAY EXPLAINS WHY ADAM WAS NEVER CURSED
                                                        ISBN: 978-1-84728-176-0

HEAVENLY ANGEL LAY LAY EXPLAINS WHY ABORTED BABIES DO NOT GO TO HEAVEN
                                                        ISBN: 978-0-6151-7470-9

HEAVENLY ANGEL LAY LAY EXPLAINS THE BIBLICAL GROUNDS FOR MARRIAGE,
          SEPARATION, AND DIVORCE   ISBN: 978-0-6151-7481-5

HEAVENLY ANGEL LAY LAY EXPLAINS WHY PROFESSIONAL COUNSELORS HAVE 'HARDENED
          HEARTS'   ISBN: 978-0-6151-7482-2

HEAVENLY ANGEL LAY LAY EXPLAINS THE DIFFERENCE BETWEEN A 'COLD CHRISTIAN' AND
          A 'BACKSLIDER'   ISBN: 978-0-6151-7483-9

HEAVENLY ANGEL LAY LAY EXPLAINS WHICH BIBLE TO READ, WHICH BIBLE NOT TO READ,
          AND WHY   ISBN: 978-0-6151-7484-6

HEAVENLY ANGEL LAY LAY EXPLAINS WHY GAYS, LESBIANS, BI-SEXUALS, AND
          TRANSSEXUALS DO NOT GO TO HEAVEN   ISBN: 978-0-6151-7485-3

HEAVENLY ANGEL LAY LAY EXPLAINS WHY CHILDREN AND SPORTS ARE DEFINITELY A
          RELIGION IN TODAY'S SOCIETY   ISBN: 978-0-6151-7486-0

HEAVENLY ANGEL LAY LAY EXPLAINS WHAT 'MANY ARE CALLED, BUT FEW ARE CHOSEN
          REALLY MEANS   ISBN: 978-0-6151-7487-7

HEAVENLY ANGEL LAY LAY AND GUARDIAN ANGEL SHADOW GUESS THE REAL AGE OF THE
          EARTH   ISBN: 978-0-6151-7488-4

AN ABUSED MAN'S BATTLES, TRYING TO PROTECT HIS BOYS   ISBN: 978-0-6151-5191-5

HEAVENLY ANGEL LAY LAY

EXPLAINS THE

<u>BIBLICAL GROUNDS</u>

<u>FOR MARRIAGE,</u>

<u>SEPARATION,</u>

<u>AND DIVORCE,</u>

ADULTERY, FORNICATION AND MARRIAGE

The following is an excerpt from my book called, **MATTHEW'S WORD 'TWO':REAL WORD OF GOD BIBLE**. This is one of the Bible Mysteries Heavenly Angel Lay Lay shared with me on our way, taking Rachael to the Promised Land. Since a Heavenly Angel told me this, how can I change anything that any Heavenly Angel said and make it better? If you don't know who Heavenly Angel Lay Lay is or how I was allowed to work with three different Heavenly Angels, then you will need to purchase **MATTHEW'S WORD 'TWO':REAL WORD OF GOD BIBLE** and read it (ISBN: 1-4116-6995-9).   The first half of **MATTHEW'S WORD 'TWO':REAL WORD OF GOD BIBLE** is about how I was allowed to work with three different Heavenly Angels to begin with. The second half of **MATTHEW'S WORD 'TWO':REAL WORD OF GOD BIBLE** contains about 100 pages of Biblical facts Heavenly Angel Lay Lay was allowed to share with me. You will need to read the whole book in order to understand how I was allowed to work with three different Heavenly Angels for a little over a year of my life. Lay Lay explained to me why Adam didn't stop Eve from eating the 'forbidden fruit', what caused Cain to get so angry he killed Abel, what happened to the Raven from Noah's Ark and why it had to be the Raven that was let out first and then the Dove, how old the Earth really is, along with other Biblical Secrets that theologians and theorists do not know.

I asked, "What does it actually take to be married in the eyes of Jesus? Does it take a Marriage License or not?" Lay Lay said, "In some countries, they don't even have a Marriage License. In the Old Testament the man and woman went and laid with each other becoming one flesh. In cultures a few years back, some 'jumped the broom' in front of friends and relatives to become husband and wife. In other cultures the man and woman actually go under a broom held by what you would call the Best Man and Brides-Maid. Then they go in a hut and consummate their marriage. The only thing they all have in common is agreeing with each other in their hearts and before Jesus they want to be man and wife and consummate their marriage. It all depends on the culture you are living in. A Marriage Certificate isn't needed for a man and a woman to become one flesh, either in the Physical World or Spiritual World, that's just a law of the land. All that is needed to become one flesh is for a man and a woman to lay with each other and agree in their hearts they wish to be man and wife in the eyes of Jesus. If it took a Marriage Certificate, then there are a lot of humans in other countries who are not married. In the United States it takes a Marriage License to be legally married, that still doesn't mean you are married before Jesus. That's why there is a legal paper called an 'Annulment', meaning the man and woman have not made love to become 'one flesh' in their marriage yet. Therefore the marriage can be made 'Void' as though it had never taken place because Biblically it actually hasn't taken place without the consummation of the marriage. The Marriage Certificate is merely legal proof that a man and woman are husband and wife, it has nothing to do with what Jesus sees taking place. A man and woman are husband and wife when they first lay together, or they are committing fornication or adultery. Yes, a Marriage License needs to be made out to follow the Laws of the Land, but if you really want to get technical, the Marriage Certificate isn't even documented for some time after the man and woman have already consummated their marriage. Does that mean they are living in sin during that time? No, the minister who married the man and woman spoke the marriage into existence through the power of the tongue and faith in his words the man and woman wanted to spend the rest of their lives together as husband and wife in their hearts, in the flesh, and in the eyes of the Living God. The man and woman proved it to Jesus through the consummation of the marriage. The Marriage Certificate is still either in the mail somewhere or sitting on the minister's desk waiting to be mailed back to the Court House. Christians are under so much pressure by 'Peer Pressure', Christians 'yield' to the culture. When the culture is doing something against the Word of God, then Christians have a Biblical Responsibility not to follow the Laws of the Land and need to stand on the Word of God. When the Laws of the Land are in agreement with the Word of God, then the Christians need to abide by both, the Word of God and the Laws of the Land. The Word of God is always first, then the Laws of the Land. God destroyed the whole Earth once, with the exception of Noah and his family, because of the wickedness of mankind not going by His Word, those humans put the Law of the Land before the Word of God just like Christians today are doing. Satan is just sitting back and laughing at them,

BIBLICAL GROUNDS FOR MARRIAGE, SEPARATION, AND DIVORCE   Page 9

enjoying all those souls he will be tormenting in Fire and Brimstone because of Christians rolling over and playing dead."

I asked, "What about a 'Prenuptial Agreement?'" Lay Lay said, "That defeats the purpose of the marriage to begin with. A marriage is based in Jesus and trust in their partner. Someone having a potential mate sign a Prenuptial Agreement is like telling the human, 'I trust you, but 'just in case' our marriage isn't going to work out I want a 'legal reassurance'.' The mate doesn't trust their potential husband or wife to begin with. Yes, a 'Prenuptial Agreement' is against the Word of God. Christians shouldn't even consider signing one. Having a potential mate sign a Prenuptial Agreement is like saying 'I love you, but my money is more important to me than you are.' The two people are actually 'unequally yoked.' We all know where the 'love of money' comes from, it's the 'root of all evil'. A Prenuptial Agreement is a legal contract just like a Marriage License, both counter-acting the other one. What good does it do to have one legal contract called a Marriage Certificate if you are going to have another legal contract called a Prenuptial Agreement to counter-act the first legal contract? That doesn't make sense, yes a Prenuptial Agreement is against the Word of the Living God."

I asked, "What about the woman Jesus forgave for being caught in the act of adultery? A lot of people think the man and woman should be forgiven time and time again." Lay Lay said, "No, Jesus told her to 'Go, and sin no more.' Jesus was giving her a second chance, just like He does everyone else. That's why Jesus said to the people 'Whoever sinneth not, casteth the first stone.' If she would have been caught in that situation again, she would have been stoned. If an adulterer or adulteress were caught in the act, they were automatically stoned to death the first time. Jesus just changed that to give the adulterer or adulteress a second chance, not a third or fourth chance. If it was a rape case and the victim was in a village or around people where he or she could yell for help and not said anything then they really weren't being raped to begin with and both of them would have been stoned. If the act happened in the wilderness where the victim could have yelled rape and there was no one around to hear their screams for 'help' then just the rapist would have been stoned, Jesus never did change that. It's all done in order to keep the Physical Bloodline clean." I said, "So technically lying with a person or having a person in your mind either over the phone as Phone Sex or over the

Page 9

computer as Cyber Sex is actually one of three things. Either a marriage to each other, if they agree to spend the rest of their lives together and do all the legal stuff to go along with it. Fornication meaning lust of the flesh, or committing adultery and actually breaking the marriage vows to someone else's marriage by laying with the man or woman who is already married to someone else. They have already had sex or made love to the person over the phone or on the computer in the eyes of Jesus." Lay Lay said, "Yes, that's right, you don't have to actually physically do the act in the flesh, like you and Detta didn't do anything in the flesh, yet you two made love together over the phone and that broke the Marriage Vows between her and Satan. Having sex over the phone or on the computer is still considered fornication or adultery in the Spiritual World if you don't intend to marry the person in the flesh." I said, "A lot of people would say, 'I don't believe that." Lay Lay said, "It doesn't matter whether the human believes it or not. Just like it doesn't matter if they believe in Jesus or not. Whether they believe it or not doesn't change the fact that it's true and on Judgment Day they will be judged accordingly. It would be better for humans to say, 'Yes, that's what the Word of God does say, the Holy Spirit, being the teacher and comforter needs to help me accept that part of His Word in my life.' That would be the honest thing to say." I said, "If that's the case, being married and divorced three times due to my ex's committing adultery against me. I have had a lot less marriages than a lot of people in the United States today. I'm sure a lot of people do that constantly on the computer and phone. They used to 'instant message' me when I was doing research for class projects. I told them I didn't believe in it and I didn't have time for it. I finally had to put some of them on 'block'." Lay Lay said, "You're right, you have had a lot less marriages than a lot of people. They aren't counting the times they have had someone on the phone or computer. A lot of them aren't even spiritually or emotionally married to who they believe their husband or wife is any longer. They are actually living in adultery with a Marriage Certificate to the one they are living with. Spiritually or emotionally they aren't married to that person any longer. They are actually spiritually married to someone they have never met in the flesh. They fell in love with the characteristics they believe the vessel has and consummated the marriage over the phone or computer. Spiritually that broke the wedding vows and consummated a new marriage. They actually love the image of the vessel they have created in their minds and hearts. Most of the time they will never meet the vessel they are spiritually married to.

There are only two Biblical reasons for divorce and one biblical reason for separation.

I. THE FIRST BIBLICAL REASON FOR DIVORCE:

1. Adultery: Matthew 5:27-32 (KJV)

27) Ye have heard that it was said by them of old time, Thou shalt not commit adultery (Voluntary sexual intercourse between a married man and someone other than his wife or between a married woman and someone other than her husband) (Merriam Webster):

28) But I say unto you, That whosoever looketh on a woman to lust (Personal inclination; usual intense or unbridled sexual desire; an intense longing; to have an intense desire to need; to have a sexual urge.) (Merriam Webster) after her hath committed adultery with her already in his heart.

29) And if thy right eye offend thee, pluck it out, and cast *it* from Thee for it is profitable for thee that one of thy members should perish, and not *that* thy whole body should be cast into hell (Until that time the member does go to Jesus, they need to be out of the membership of a church; not pushed out the door of the church, because that's when they really need the Christian to care about and help them, but not to allow the person authority over the members of the church. Just like Rick, one little sin leads to another and another, and the sin's get worse. Pretty quick that little 'lust' is actually having sex with women in the church like Pastor Lee. Then the person goes on and does more, deeper sin, like the Israelites. Pretty soon that person isn't serving Jesus Christ of Nazareth from their hearts any longer, but Satan. That's why Jesus said that, He knew once one sin from the flesh starts, if it isn't stopped, it will go to the heart and pretty soon the heart isn't serving Jesus any longer. Not only will the sin continue by the person doing the sin, but it will affect their husband or wife and children as well. The sin keeps growing.).

30) And if thy right hand offend thee, cut it off, and cast *it* from thee: for it is profitable for thee that one of thy members should perish, and not *that* thy whole body should be cast into hell.

31) It hath been said, Whosoever shall put away his wife, let him give her a writing of divorcement:

32) But I say unto you, That whosoever shall put away his wife, saving for the case of fornication, causeth her to commit adultery: and whosoever shall marry her that is divorced committeth adultery.

Matthew 19:9 (KJV)
9) And I say unto you, Whosoever shall put away his wife, except *it be* for fornication (Consensual sexual intercourse between two persons not married to each other.) (Merriam Webster), and shall marry another, committeth adultery: And whoso marrieth her which is put away doth commit adultery."

Mark 10:1-12 (KJV)
1) And he arose from thence, and commeth into the coasts of Judaea by the farther side of Jordan: and the people resort unto him again; and, as he was wont, he taught them again.
2) And the Pharisees came to him, and asked him, Is it lawful for a man to put away *his* wife? Tempting him.
3) And he answered and said unto them, 'What did Moses command you?'
4) And they said, Moses suffered to write a bill of divorcement [Here is an interesting verse. Even back before the times of Jesus Christ. The people were to have the Divorce Papers in their hands **before** the woman was removed from that household. It gave the couple a chance to reconcile (Come to a mutual understanding according to the Word of God) their differences and not go through with the divorce], and to put *her* away.
5) And Jesus answered and said unto them, 'For the hardness of your heart he wrote you this precept.
6) But from the beginning of the creation God made them male and female.
7) For this cause shall a man leave his father and mother, and cleave to his wife;
8) And they twain shall be one flesh: so then they are no more twain, but one flesh.
9) What therefore God hath joined together, let not man put asunder.'
10) And in the house his disciples asked him again of the same *matter*.
11) And he saith unto them, 'Whosoever shall put away his wife, and marry another, committeth adultery against her.
12) And if a woman shall put away her husband, and be married to

another, she committeth adultery.

Luke 16:15-18 (KJV)

15) And he said unto them, 'Ye are they which justify yourselves before men; but God knoweth your hearts: for that which is highly esteemed among men is abomination in the sight of God.

16) **The law and the prophets *were* until John: <u>SINCE THAT TIME</u>** <u>the kingdom of God is preached, **and every man presseth into it**</u>.

17) And it is easier for heaven and earth to pass, than one tittle (Don't remove the meaning of even one word from the Word of God. The Word of God will remain until after heaven and earth pass. All those 'false doctrines' won't ever change what the Word of God says.) of the law to fail,

18) Whosoever putteth away his wife, and marrieth another, committeth adultery: and whosoever marrieth her that is put away from *her* husband committeth adultery."

I said, "Some women would say, 'That scripture means a man can't divorce a woman, but a woman can divorce a man." Lay Lay said, "No, the 'man' is the masculine tense for either sex. It's just the independent women who say that or someone else the human knows who wants to try to find a 'loop hole' in the Word of God for themselves or someone else."

Lay Lay continued, "1 Corinthians 7:1-16 (KJV)

1) Now concerning the things whereof ye wrote unto me: *It is* good for a man not to touch a woman.

2) Nevertheless, *to avoid* fornication, let every man have his own wife, and let every woman have her own husband.

3) Let the husband render unto the wife due benevolence: and likewise also the wife unto the husband.

4) The wife hath not power of her own body, but the husband: and likewise also the husband hath not power of his own body, but the wife.

5) <u>**Defraud ye not one the other, EXCEPT *IT BE* WITH CONSENT**</u> <u>**for a time,** that ye may give yourselves to fasting and prayer, and come together again, that Satan tempt you not for your incontinency.</u> (Man and woman agreeing to the separation.)

Like if the husband and wife goes for up to Camp Meeting for a week, but only to get closer to Jesus Christ because of the Camp Meeting. (BIBLICAL REASON FOR SEPARATION.)

6) But I speak this by permission, *and* not of commandment.

7) For I would that all men were even as I myself. But every man hath his proper gift of God, one after this manner, and another after that.

8) I say therefore to the unmarried and widows, It is good for them if they abide even as I.

9) But if they cannot contain, let them marry: for it is better to marry than to burn.

10) And unto the married I command, *yet* not I, but the Lord, Let not the wife depart from *her* husband:

11) But and if she depart, let her remain unmarried, or be reconciled to *her* husband: and not the husband put away *his* wife,

12) But to the rest speak I, not the Lord: If any brother hath a wife that believeth not, and she be pleased to dwell with him, let him not put her away.

II. THE SECOND BIBLICAL REASON FOR DIVORCE:

      2) and when the 'unsanctified' chooses to leave the 'sanctified'.

13) And the woman which hath an husband that believeth not, and if he be pleased to dwell with her, let her not leave him.

14) For the unbelieving husband is sanctified by the wife, and the unbelieving wife is sanctified by the husband: else were your children unclean; but now are they holy.

15) But **if the unbelieving depart, let him depart. A brother or a sister is not under bondage in such cases,** but God hath called us to peace.

WHY. IN ORDER TO SAVE THE UNSAVED:

1 Corinthians 7:16 For what knowest thou, O wife, whether **THOU SHALT SAVE THY HUSBAND**? or how knowest thou, O man, whether **THOU SHALT SAVE THY WIFE**? (You notice this scripture says it's up to the saved spouse to save the unsaved spouse?)

III.   THIS   IS   THE   ONLY   BIBLICAL   REASON   FOR 'SEPARATION': for a husband and wife and only then for a short period of time **with each other's consent.** There is no other biblical reason for 'separation.

I Corinthians 7:5

5) Defraud ye not one the other, EXCEPT *IT BE* WITH CONSENT for a time, **that ye may give yourselves to fasting and prayer, and come together again, that Satan tempt you not for your incontinency.** (Both people agreeing to the separation.)

Like if the husband and wife goes for up to Camp Meeting for a week, but only to get closer to Jesus because of the Camp Meeting."

Lay Lay said, "If the separation or divorce isn't for those reasons to begin with, it's against the Word of God and a sin." I asked, "So, a Restraining Order is against the Word of God?" Lay Lay said, "Yes, a Restraining Order is against the Word of God. A Restraining Order is a legal form that contradicts another legal form called the Marriage Certificate and their Wedding Vows. It's hard enough for a husband and wife to go for the length of a Camp Meeting without being intimate and being able to talk to each other about family issues in private, not to mention for any length of time over three to five days, especially when the couple is first married. Restraining Orders are just Satan's way of not allowing a husband and wife to work out their problems together and talking to each other. A Restraining Order would be like a Christian not talking to Jesus intimately for a lengthy period of time, usually a year. They forget His voice and start listening to someone other than Jesus. That's how a lot of men and women start committing adultery if they aren't already doing so at the time of separation, they get lonely and most men and women their age are already busy with their own families so they go out of the church realm to look for companionship, they find companionship in more ways than one. A husband and wife needs to be able to communicate with each other or the marriage will be over, just like Christians need to talk to Jesus daily or their walk with Him suffers. Restraining Orders are Satan's trick to get husbands and wives legally battling each other instead of battling the influences outside the family, it causes hatred and unforgiveness. At times State agencies take the children away, then they tell either the husband or wife, it's usually the wife, Satan working on the emotions again, if she puts a Restraining Order on her husband the state will give her children back to her faster. That's the legal term for 'Ransom'. So she chooses the children over the husband. If the husband and wife commit to working out their problems instead of fighting each other they would be able to keep their family, Foster Care wouldn't even come into the picture." That's 180 degrees opposite a loving spouse and family values Jesus wants everyone to have."

I asked, "Is it good for a child to be in Foster Care?" Lay Lay said, "It's never good when children have to be separated from their natural parents unless that parent is forcing the child to do things against the Word of God. If one parent is going against the Word of God, such as having sex with a child behind the other parents back, then the parent needs to leave the parent having sex with the child to begin with and divorce that parent. They have Biblical grounds for divorce due to adultery and incest as well. As far as putting children somewhere, it's never good for anyone especially Christians to have their child in Foster Care. There are always relatives or families from the church that could take a child in for a night or two if it's needed. Just look at what happened with the Foster Boys at Pastor Lee's house? That could have been someone else's son or daughter those boys had sex with or it could have been girls having sex with the children in Foster Care as well. Other children in Foster Care could actually be possessed with demons like Lillith forcing other children to do things that no child should go through. Just because Detta allowed it due to her background doesn't mean the boys wouldn't have forced another boy or girl to have sex with them, those boys would have raped him or her. The only thing the Foster Parents would have happen to them is most states, after an investigation, if the Foster Parents are found to be at fault, is to loose their Foster Care License. Then the state would cover the incident up because the Foster Care House is 'Licensed' by the State. The parent may never have known, especially if the boy or girl was a very young age and couldn't speak out or afraid to speak out and tell what happened to him or her. The Foster Boys in Pastor Lee's house have had sex with other children in Foster Care before. You could tell that by the way Detta said, 'They looked at me, then they looked at each other and smirked.' Some other child could easily get possessed by an 'unclean spirit' in Foster Care. The parents wouldn't know anything about it. The states would deny being 'possessed by an unclean spirit' is even possible. The parents would have to prove somehow the child is not only possessed, but the possession happened while in the care of the state. It could take a month or more for the 'unclean spirit' to even go into the vessel depending on the type of the 'unclean spirit'.

The characteristics of the 'unclean spirit' have to change the characteristics of the vessel first to the characteristics of Satan, then the vessel has the characteristics of Satan, just like when the girls were bitten by the Vampire Unclean Spirit, then the 'unclean spirit' needs to change the characteristics of the vessel to those specific characteristics of the 'unclean spirit' itself. The 'unclean spirit' could just latch onto the vessel and stay there for a while. The child would still have the characteristics of the 'unclean spirit' going through the child. Like Lillith, if she were to do that to a child. Lillith would want sex with any man she could get. Once the parents get the child back, the child would even take sex with the father or mother and if the parents didn't give Lillith, or Syenson the male unclean spirit with the characteristics of sexual desire, what the demon wanted, all the demon would have to do is claim the parent tried to 'molest' the vessel, even though that wasn't the case. Then the police and Social Services would arrest the parent just on the word of the child while an investigation goes on. The parent would have to either give into Lillith or Syenson and have sex with the child or prove somehow there is an 'unclean spirit' in the child.

Razon would start cutting the wrists of the child, the child would be legally marked as 'suicidal' and there is no way for the parent to prove otherwise. Yet, the child was fine when the state came in and took the child. The state would cover it up because it's 'confidential'. Not only Christian families, but all families who have problems need to see Pastor Lee's house as a real example of what happens in Foster Care. When children get involved in the state laws, the parents have no say in what church the Foster Care Parents take their children to, if any at all, or how their own children are being raised to believe or act. The states can't regulate what goes on in Foster Parents Homes. That's considered 'Separation between Church and State', although it really isn't. Human's just think it is because of the media. The family may have Ouija Boards in the house, hold séances, Satan's play toys for children, all kinds of things. It would be better to keep the children where the parents are and work out their differences through their minister or talk their differences out between themselves. There are children in Foster Care Homes that's been there for years, being moved from one home to another without the parents knowledge, that's all considered Confidential and kept secret, that's not stability. Those are years without the parents being able to make decisions in their own children's lives. In Foster Care the parents are leaving life long decisions for their own children up to total strangers whom they know nothing about. Yes, State Counselors may say, 'It'll only be a few days before the hearing', but State Counselors aren't the ones wearing the Black Robe called judges either,. State Counselors can't guarantee anything, State Counselors only tell parents what they want parents to know. They don't tell parents the judges will keep their children in Foster Care indefinitely. State Counselors don't tell parents the judges may order the children to stay in Foster Care until the parents go through a year of counseling with secular counselors not being allowed to bring the name of Jesus or the Word of God into the counseling sessions, Satan is deceiving. Those who enforce such laws whether they support the laws or not, Christian or non-Christian alike are guilty of breaking up that marriage and family. Just like the Board Members, Senate, House of Representatives, Presidents, Counselors, Attorneys, Judges, Parliaments, Kings, and Queens are being used by Satan today. Jesus never gave children to parents for someone else to raise, it's not the will of Jesus the children are in Foster Care, it's Satan tricking parents and society out of letting the parents raise their own children.   Satanists women in the villages are forced to put their own children in cottages not knowing how their children are being raised, not even knowing their own children. State laws force parents to do the same thing in Foster Care not knowing how or having any say in how their own children are being raised for months or even years, most with just Supervised Visitation. What's 180% difference from a broken heart, broken marriages, and not being able to have any say in how your own children are raised? The happy life with everything to say about how your children are being raised. Jesus wants His children to have a loving family with everything to say about how their children are raised."

ILLITERACY IN THE UNITED STATES

Lay Lay asked, "I know you have a Bachelor's Degree in Psychology and two minors. One in Counseling and one in Religion, but what is your Accumulated Grade Point Average? I said, "It's around a 2.26.   That's why no Master's Program will accept me.   I did get a temporary admittance into one seminary in Springfield, Missouri, but I couldn't afford the first semester of their 'temporary admittance' so I couldn't go. Lay Lay asked, "What happened?" I said, "To begin with I can pretty much tell you what the 'theorists' believe, but my mind isn't differentiating them one from the other so I get the theories mixed up. Second, There was one in particular instructor who I just couldn't understand. I went to ask him a few questions and he talked so far above me that my mind wasn't able to comprehend what he was saying." Lay Lay said, "Yes, that's why there is so much illiteracy in the United States today. Teachers have the idea that the student is supposed to go up to the teacher's level when in all actuality the teacher needs to be able to get down to the student's level. Some students can't get up to the teacher's level, their mind just doesn't function that way, like yours. Just like Jesus had to come down to human level for everyone to be 'saved'. He knew that it was impossible for the human to get up to His level, so He came to their level. When a teacher can get down to the student's level, that's when a teacher is a good teacher and can get their point across to all the students, not just a select few."

ABRAHAM

AND

SARAH

(CONTINUED FROM:
ABRAHAM AND SARAH PART 1 IN
HEAVENLY ANGEL LAY LAY EXPLAINS WHY
ABORTED BABIES DO NOT GO TO HEAVEN)

After I tell the reader Biblical Facts that Heavenly Angel Lay Lay told me when I was working with her and Shadow, I will be writing about different stories from the King James Version of the Word of God talking about the family aspects in the Word of God. How the different couples in the bible met, what the couples went through, and what men, women, and children are commanded to do and not to do according to the Word of God. Just like HEAVENLY ANGEL LAY LAY taught me how to do.

ABRAHAM AND SARAH

Genesis 25:1-10
1) Then again Abraham took a wife, and her name was Keturah.
2) And she bare him Zimran, and Jokshan, and Medan, and Midian, and Ishbak, and Shuah.
3) And Jokshan begat Sheba, and Dedan. And the sons of Dedan were Asshurim, and Letushim, and Leummim.
4) And the sons of Midian; Ephah, and Epher, and Hanoch, and Abidah, and Eldaah. All these were the children of Keturah.
5) And Abraham gave all that he had unto Isaac.
6) But unto the sons of the concubines, which Abraham had, Abraham gave gifts, and sent them away from Isaac his son, while he yet lived, eastward, unto the east country. (Now Isaac is in Hebron where Sarah was buried)

Genesis 22:1-24 continued (I put these scriptures here because 20 says, 'it came to pass', meaning 'eventually', a long time went by before he was told these things. According to the ages of each individual and dates of each event this happened after Sarah's death and Abraham's remarriage)
20) And it came to pass after these things (eventually), that it was told Abraham (Someone Abraham knew well and trusted had to have seen him

and told him), saying, Behold, Milcah, she hath also born children unto thy brother Nahor;

21) Huz his firstborn, and Buz his brother, and Kemuel the father of Aram,

22) And Chesed, and Hazo, and Pildash, and Jidlaph, and Bethuel.

23) And Bethuel begat Rebekah: these eight Milcah did bear to Nahor, Abraham's brother.

24) And his concubine, whose name was Reumah, she bare also Tebah, and Gaham, and Thahash, and Maachah

Genesis 24:1-5

1) And Abraham was old, and well stricken in age: and the LORD had blessed Abraham in all things.

2) And Abraham said unto his eldest servant of his house, that ruled over all that he had, Put, I pray thee, thy hand under my thigh: (The steward of the house is Eliezer of Damascus) (Genesis 15:2)

3) And I will make thee swear by the LORD, the God of heaven, and the God of the earth, that thou shalt not take a wife unto my son of the daughters of the Canaanites, (Abraham is still in Canaan. Isaac and his wife would be 'unequally yoked' and the 'sanctified, Abraham's son, Isaac would be bound to the 'unsanctified', his wife who didn't worship the Lord) among whom I dwell:

Deuteronomy 7:3

3) Neither shalt thou (you) make marriages with them; thy (your) daughter thou (you) shalt not give unto his son, nor his daughter shalt thou (you) take unto thy (your) son.

Joshua 23:12-13

12) Else if ye (you) do in any wise go back, and cleave (cling) unto the remnant (survivors) of these nations, *even* these that remain (survivors) among you, and shall make marriages with them, and go in unto them, and they to you:

13) Know for a certainty that the LORD your God will no more drive out *any of* these nations from before you (will no longer help you); but they shall be snares and traps unto you, and scourges (open wounds) in your sides, and thorns in your eyes, until ye (you) perish from off this good land which the LORD your God hath given you.

1 Kings 11:2

2) Of the nations *concerning* which the LORD said unto the children of Israel, Ye (you) shall not go in to them, neither shall they come in unto you: *for* surely they will turn away your heart after their gods (make you true 'backsliders'): Solomon clave unto these in love (turned to 'false gods').

Exodus 34:16

16) And thou (you) take of their daughters unto thy (your) sons, and their daughters go a-whoring after their gods (serving several 'false gods'), and make thy (your) sons go a-whoring after their gods (turning their back on God and serve 'false gods' instead because their daughters serve 'false gods').

4) But thou shalt go unto my country (That would be Ur of the Chaldees), and to my kindred, and take a wife unto my son Isaac.

5) And the servant said unto him, Peradventure the woman will not be willing to follow me unto this land: must I needs bring thy son again unto the land from whence (where) thou camest (Ur, where Abraham was from) (If the woman won't come to Isaac in this new land, should I take Isaac to her)? (Abraham's servant is going to get Rebekah now)

6) And Abraham said unto him, Beware thou (you) that thou (you) **bring not my son thither (there) again** [(No, don't take Isaac to her. This was said twice, once here and once in verse 8).

7) The LORD God of heaven, which took me from my father's house, and from the land of my kindred (kin), and which spake unto me, and that sware (promised) unto me, saying, Unto thy seed will I give this land; he shall send his angel before thee (you), and thou shalt take a wife unto my son from thence (there).

8) And if the woman will not be willing to follow thee (you), then thou shalt be clear from this my oath: **only bring not my son thither (there) again** (Do not take Isaac to her. Abraham was so insistent on this issue, Abraham knew God had promised Abraham that the land Abraham was living in was meant for Abraham's off spring and Abraham's off spring would be too numerous to count)

Continuing in Genesis 24:37, 62, 67 when the servant goes for Rebekah. I had to overlap these two stories a little to finish Abraham and Sarah and keep Isaac and Rebekah complete.

37) And my master made me swear, saying, Thou shalt not take a wife to

my son of the daughters of the <u>Canaanites, in whose land I dwell</u>: (This tells us Abraham is in Beersheba, not in Gerar, Beersheba is in Canaan. Now on Rebekah's journey to Isaac, after Sarah was dead, Rebekah asked all kinds of questions about Isaac and his family, the servant told Rebekah everything, including that time period that Hagar and Ishmael was kicked out)

62) And <u>Isaac came from the way of the well Lahairoi</u>; for <u>he dwelt in the south country</u> (Isaac is all grown up now, living in Kadesh-Barnea, visiting Ishmael. Ishmael is in the Wilderness of Paran, close to his mother Hagar in Egypt, remember?).

67) And Isaac brought her (Rebekah) into <u>his mother Sarah's tent</u> and took (laid with, made love to) Rebekah, and she became his wife (Nothing else was required to have a marriage); and he loved her: and Isaac was comforted (by Rebekah) after his mother's death (Sarah had been dead for three years and Abraham had remarried. That's why the scripture is very specific about the tent belonging to Sarah, the tent didn't belong to Abraham or Abraham's second wife, Keturah. Rebekah had no idea when Isaac took her into the tent whose tent it used to be, she also didn't have any idea Isaac didn't know the role Sarah had in kicking Hagar and Ishmael out. As far as Rebekah knew, Isaac was already aware about Sarah's role in this whole thing. It was only after the consummation of the marriage that Isaac and Rebekah started talking and Rebekah told Isaac what the servant told her about Sarah making Abraham kick Hagar and Ishmael out and into the Wilderness of Paran. Remember, the scriptures say Isaac and Rebekah met in the field and they went straight to the tent and took Rebekah for his wife. They didn't sit around talking for a while, they immediately consummated their marriage. It was only after Rebekah was his wife that Isaac found out. What a way to start a marriage. Rebekah started out being a good wife to Isaac, she told her husband the whole truth as it was told to her. It wouldn't be hard for Isaac to have the facts confirmed by one of the servants who were there at the time if Isaac felt that was necessary. Remember, Isaac, at the time Hagar and Ishmael were kicked out, was still a little boy. One night Isaac went to bed and had a playmate, the next morning Isaac woke up and the playmate and the playmate's mother were gone, just like Heavenly Angel Lay Lay said, eventually the child will find out the truth, even if the truth comes out in their adulthood).

Genesis 25:20
20) And <u>Isaac was forty years old when he took Rebekah to wife</u>, the daughter of Bethuel the Syrian of Padanaram, the sister to Laban the Syrian. (Here are the age facts. Abraham was 86 when Ishmael was born, that made Sarah 96, Abraham was 10 years older than Sarah. Abraham was 100, Sarah was 90, and Ishmael was 14 when Isaac was born. Remember, Abraham and Ishmael were both circumcised the same day, Abraham was 99 and Ishmael was 13. It was the very next year that Sarah gave birth to Isaac. Sarah was 127 when she died, Abraham was 137, Ishmael was 51, and Isaac was 37. Sarah had been dead three years now before Isaac and Rebekah were married. Isaac didn't take Rebekah to marry until he was 40. Abraham was 140, and Ishmael was 54 when Isaac and Rebekah were married. Abraham was 175 when he died, Ishmael was 89, and Isaac was 75 when they buried Abraham)

Genesis 25:1-10 continued
7) And these are the days of the years of Abraham's life which he lived, an hundred threescore and fifteen years. (175 years old when Abraham died)
8) Then Abraham gave up the ghost, and died in a good old age, an old man, and full of years; and was gathered to his people.
9) And his sons Isaac (75 years old) and Ishmael (89 years old) buried him in the cave of Machpelah, in the field of Ephron the son of Zohar the Hittite, which is before Mamre;
10) The field which Abraham purchased of the sons of Heth: there was Abraham buried, and Sarah his wife.
11) And it came to pass after the death of Abraham, that God blessed his son Isaac; and Isaac dwelt by the well Lahairoi (Isaac moved to around Kadesh-Barnea. Close to the Paran Desert where Ishmael lived, on the border of the Wilderness of Paran. This is how Ishmael knew Abraham had died, Isaac told him. They lived close to each other and visited each other. That's also why later on in scriptures and in my book about Isaac and Rebekah with Esau and Jacob that Isaac and Rebekah were sick when they found out Esau took a daughter of Ishmael's, they both knew Ishmael and his wife out of Egypt were 'idol worshippers' and Isaac and Rebekah's son marrying Ishmael's daughter makes Isaac and Rebekah's son 'unequally yoked'. A Christian marrying a non-Christian).

Genesis 26:1-6, 17

1) And there was a famine in the land, beside the first famine that was in the days of Abraham. And Isaac went unto Abimelech king of the Philistines unto Gerar.

2) <u>And the LORD appeared unto him, and said, Go not down into Egypt; dwell in the land which I shall tell thee of:</u>

3) <u>Sojourn (temporary stay) in this land, and I will be with thee, and will bless thee; for unto thee, and unto thy seed, I will give all these countries, and I will perform the oath which I sware unto Abraham thy father;</u>

4) <u>And I will make thy seed to multiply as the stars of heaven, and will give unto thy seed all these countries; and in thy seed shall all the nations of the earth be blessed;</u>

5) <u>Because that Abraham obeyed my voice, and kept my charge, my commandments, my statutes, and my laws.</u> (This is God's half of the covenant to Isaac. If we don't keep His commandments and do as He says, we don't get His blessings)

6) <u>And Isaac dwelt in Gerar:</u>

17) <u>And Isaac departed thence (from there), and pitched **his** tent in the valley of Gerar, and dwelt there.</u> (Now Isaac's half of the covenant between Isaac and God. Isaac is back in the Philistines. You notice that <u>the scriptures say 'pitched his tent', not 'his mother Sarah's tent' this time</u>. That tells us that Isaac found out the truth about what Sarah did and then is when he moved to Kadesh-Barnea close to the Wilderness of Paran where Ishmael and his wife lived)

ABRAHAM

MARRIES

AGAIN

ABRAHAM MARRIES AGAIN

Genesis 25:1-10

1) Then again Abraham took a wife, and her name *was* Keturah. (This is only after Sarah had died)

2) And she bare him Zimran, and Jokshan, and Medan, and Midian, and Ishbak, and Shuah.

3) And Jokshan begat Sheba, and Dedan. And the sons of Dedan were Asshurim, and Letushim, and Leummim.

4) And the sons of Midian; Ephah, and Epher, and Hanoch, and Abidah, and Eldaah. All these *were* the children of Keturah.

5) And Abraham gave all that he had unto Isaac. (The first-born son gets all the inheritance. Abraham's second wife doesn't inherit anything nor do any of the children of Abraham's second wife. Ishmael is not considered Abraham's son by God)

6) But unto the sons of the concubines, which Abraham had, Abraham gave gifts, and sent them away from Isaac his son, while he yet lived, eastward, unto the east country. (Abraham releasing all his servants before he died. Isaac didn't inherit them)

7) And these *are* the days of the years of Abraham's life which he lived, an hundred threescore and fifteen years (175 years).

8) Then Abraham gave up the ghost, and died in a good old age, an old man, and full *of years;* and was gathered to his people.

9) And his sons Isaac and Ishmael buried him in the cave of Machpelah, in the field of Ephron the son of Zohar the Hittite, which *is* before Mamre;

10) The field which Abraham purchased of the sons of Heth: there was Abraham buried, and Sarah his wife.

11) And it came to pass after the death of Abraham, that God blessed his son Isaac; and Isaac dwelt by the well Lahairoi. (God continued to bless Isaac, the first born son, over and above what Abraham left Isaac)

ISAAC

AND

REBEKAH

ISAAC AND REBEKAH

Genesis 24:1-67

1) And Abraham was old, and well stricken in age: and the LORD had blessed Abraham in all things.

2) And Abraham said unto his eldest servant of his house, that ruled over all that he had, Put, I pray thee, thy hand under my thigh: [The steward of the house is Eliezer of Damascus (Genesis 15:2)]

3) And I will make thee swear by the LORD, the God of heaven, and the God of the earth, that thou shalt not take a wife unto my son of the daughters of the Canaanites [[(Abraham is still in Canaan. Isaac and his wife would be 'unequally yoked' and the 'sanctified. Abraham's son, Isaac would be bound to the unsanctified), his wife who didn't worship the Lord]', among whom I dwell:

Deuteronomy 7:3

3) Neither shalt thou (you) make marriages with them; thy (your) daughter thou (you) shalt not give unto his son, nor his daughter shalt thou (you) take unto thy (your) son.

Joshua 23:12-13

12) Else if ye (you) do in any wise go back, and cleave (cling) unto the remnant (survivors) of these nations, *even* these that remain (survivors) among you, and shall make marriages with them, and go in unto them, and they to you:

13) Know for a certainty that the LORD your God will no more drive out *any of* these nations from before you (Will no longer help you); but they shall be snares and traps unto you, and scourges (open wounds) in your sides, and thorns in your eyes, until ye (you) perish from off this good land which the LORD your God hath given you.

1 Kings 11:2

2) Of the nations *concerning* which the LORD said unto the children of Israel, Ye (you) shall not go in to them, neither shall they come in unto you: *for* surely they will turn away your heart after their gods (make you true 'backsliders'): Solomon clave unto these in love (turned to 'false gods').

Exodus 34:16

16) And thou (you) take of their daughters unto thy (your)

sons, and their daughters go a-whoring after their gods (serving several 'false gods'), and make thy (your) sons go a-whoring after their gods (turning their back on God and serve 'false gods' instead because their daughters serve 'false gods').

4) But thou (you) shalt go unto my country (Ur of Chaldees) , and to my kindred, and take a wife unto (for) my son Isaac.

5) And the servant said unto him (Abraham), Peradventure the woman will not be willing to follow me unto this land: must I needs bring thy (your) son again unto the land from whence (where) thou camest (Ur, where Abraham was from) (If the woman won't come to Isaac in this new land, should I take Isaac to her)?

6) And Abraham said unto him, Beware thou (you) that thou (you) **bring not my son thither (there) again** [(No, don't take Isaac to her. This was said twice, once here and once in verse 8).

7) The LORD God of heaven, which took me from my father's house, and from the land of my kindred (kin, blood relatives), and which spake unto me, and that sware (promised) unto me, saying, Unto thy seed will I give this land; he shall send his angel before thee (you), and thou shalt take a wife unto my son from thence (there).

8) And if the woman will not be willing to follow thee (you), then thou shalt be clear from this my oath: **only bring not my son thither (there) again** (Do not take Isaac to her. Abraham was so insistent on this issue, Abraham knew God had promised Abraham that Abraham's seed would be too numerous to count)

9) And the servant put his hand under the thigh of Abraham his master, and sware (promised) to him concerning that matter (To bring back a wife for Isaac).

10) And the servant took **ten camels** of the **camels of his master** (Meaning Abraham had many more camels than just ten), and departed; for all the goods of his master were in his hand (The servant took whatever he needed for the trip and loaded all the good on the backs of the camels, nine camels worth of goods. Right now we know the servant had to have at least one camel to ride on. We find out later there are other men that went on the journey with this servant, so we can assume there were nine camels that had men on them along with all the provisions of the journey. By the time they arrived at their destination all the provisions would have been used up and they would have had to purchase more food

and provisions 'for the journey back): and he arose, and went to Mesopotamia (a country), unto the city of Nahor.

In Genesis 16:3) And Sarai Abram's wife took Hagar her maid the Egyptian, after Abram had dwelt ten years in the land of **Canaan**, and gave her to her husband Abram to be his wife [Now we also know the servant's journey started in the land of Canaan and was going to Nahor, a city in Mesopotamia to get Isaac's wife. Mesopotamia is between the Tigris and Euphrates Rivers in modern day Turkey. The approximate distance between Canaan and Mesopotamia is 700 miles, 3500 kilometers (1 kilometer = 0.62 miles. The number for the kilometer is higher than the number for the mile) (700 miles/0.62 = 3500 kilometers) from Canaan to Mesopotamia. Let's keep in mind that these figures are straight line measurements and the terrain is either rocky hills or sandy with dunes so either way the journey was not just a straight line, there were valleys and hills the camels had to travel through making the distance a lot longer. Each camel being weighed down with a very heavy load could carry 450 kg/990 lbs, the camel works only six to eight months of the year, so the journey to her country and back would have had to be during that time period. The rest of the time out of the year, the camel needs to rest and recuperate. A working camel can go about 25 miles or 40 kilometers a day. So it took approximately ten weeks (14 days) of hard travel to get to Isaac's future wife's country, that's just one way. We also need to remember they rested on the seventh day, in other words, no one went anywhere on the seventh day. A camel can drink 100 litres/21 gallons of water in ten minutes, which is stored in their bloodstream. Each gallon of water weighs 8 lbs. Each camel could carry 124 gallons of water. If the camels were just carrying their minimum load weight, they wouldn't have been able to carry all the provisions, water, and men that it would have taken to take this journey. We also need to remember that on the journey back there was the bride to be along with all the servants on the camels. So the time of the journey back would have had to have been longer than the time to get to her country to begin with. The servant did leave her family with gifts so some of the weight would have been gone. The tent, cooking stuff, bedding, and other provisions would have still been on the camels, etc. We are looking at least a ten week journey to her country and at least ten weeks back home to get to Isaac]. Now we also know the servant's journey started in Hebron, Canaan. We get this from Genesis

23:19)

Genesis 23:19) And after this, Abraham buried Sarah his wife in the cave of the field of Machpelah before Mamre: the same is Hebron in the land of Canaan. [(From Hebron, Canaan to Nahor, a city in Mesopotamia to get Isaac's wife. Mesopotamia is between the Tigris and Euphrates Rivers in modern day Turkey. The approximate distance between Hebron, Canaan and Nahor, Mesopotamia. I'm going to use Ur instead of Nahor because Ur is actually on a map. <u>It will still give you an idea which is what these figures are supposed to do, **just give you an idea of what everyone went through**</u>). From Hebron to Damascus is about 160 miles or 167.2 kilometers north and from Damascus to Mari is about 300 miles or 501 kilometers north east and Mari to Ur is about 400 miles or 668 kilometers east. From Hebron to Ur is 160+300+400=860 miles or 167.2+501+668=1,336.2 kilometers north-east. 1.67 kilometer=1 mile (Merriam-Webster) The number for the kilometer is higher than the number for the mile. Each camel being weighed down with a very heavy load could carry 450 kg/990 lbs (Merriam-Webster), the camel works only six to eight months of the year (Merriam-Webster), so the journey to her country and back would have had to be during that time period. The rest of the time out of the year, the camel needs to rest and recuperate. A working camel can go about 25 miles or 41.75 kilometers a day (Merriam-Webster). So it took approximately 34.4 days/6 days a week=5.7 weeks to get to Ur from Hebron. We also need to remember they rested on the seventh day, in other words, no one went anywhere on the seventh day, that's why I divide the numbers by six instead of seven. A camel can drink 100 litres/21 gallons of water in ten minutes, which is stored in their bloodstream. Each gallon of water weighs 8 lbs. Each camel could carry 124 gallons of water. If the camels were just carrying their minimum load weight, they wouldn't have been able to carry all the provisions, water, and men that it would have taken to take this journey. We also need to remember that on the journey back there was the bride to be along with all the servants on the camels. So the time of the journey back would have had to have been longer than the time to get to her country to begin with. The servant did leave her family with gifts so some of the weight would have been gone. The tent, cooking stuff, bedding, and other provisions would have still been on the camels, etc. We are looking at least an eight week journey to her country and at least eight weeks back home to get to

Isaac]

11) And he (the servant) made his camels to kneel down without (outside of) the city by a well of water at the time of the evening, even the time that women go out to draw water.

12) And he (the servant) said O LORD God of my master Abraham, I pray thee (ask you), send me good speed (quickly) this day, and shew (show) kindness unto my master Abraham.

13) Behold, I stand here by the well of water; and the daughters of the men of the city come out to draw water:

14) And let it come to pass, that the damsel to whom I shall say, Let down thy (your) pitcher, I pray (ask) thee (you), that I may drink; and she shall say, Drink, and I will give thy (your) camels drink also: let the same be she that thou (you) hast (have) appointed for thy (your) servant Isaac; and thereby shall I know that thou (you) hast (have) shewed (shown) kindness unto my master. (Now, this is very important for all the women today who are praying for husbands and wanting confirmation about the man that Jesus is sending to them. Abraham didn't ask for a sign or a confirmation, Isaac didn't ask for a sign or a confirmation, the servant asked for a sign, but not a confirmation)

15) And it came to pass, before he had done speaking, that, behold, Rebekah came out, who was born to Bethuel, son of Milcah, the wife of Nahor, Abraham's brother, with her pitcher upon her shoulder.

16) And the damsel was **very fair to look upon** (she was good looking), a virgin, neither had any man known her (Making the point that Rebekah was a virgin twice): and she went down to the well, and filled her pitcher, and came up.

17) And the servant ran to meet her (Rebekah), and said, Let me, I pray thee (ask of you), drink a little water of thy (from your) pitcher.

18) And she (Rebekah) said, Drink, my lord (the servant): and she hasted (hurried), and let down her pitcher upon her hand, and gave him drink.

19) And when she had done giving him drink, she said, I will draw water for thy (your) camels also, until they (the camels) have done drinking (Now remember how much water even one camel can drink? That's a lot of water. Now here is the sign that the servant wanted, no confirmation was ever given by any third party as so many women today want from Jesus Christ. Did the sign come from the woman's friend, the woman's father or mother, or the woman's brother or sister? No, the sign came

from the woman herself because that's who the servant ask the sign to come from and there is no confirmation. Did the woman ask for confirmation? No. There is no where in scriptures that the woman ever asked for any confirmation. Also, this woman knows the value of camels, she offered to give the camels to drink knowing they are very valuable. A good family woman for any man who desires a family, or in their culture with a lot of valuable animals and precious items making sure the assets of this servants master's family is protected).

20) And <u>she</u> (Rebekah) <u>hasted</u> (She RAN, HURRIED, she knew the camels were very thirsty and they needed lots of water fast), and emptied her pitcher into the trough, and **ran** <u>again unto the well to draw water, and drew for all his camels</u> (The camels were drinking water so fast she had to run to draw water and get enough water back to the trough for all the camels to drink. She had to draw for ten camels and remember how much water each camel can drink and how fast each camel can drink a gallon of water?).

21) And the man wondering at her (watching her) held his peace (didn't say a word), to wit (wondering) whether the LORD had made his journey prosperous or not (The servant was waiting on the LORD for the answer).

22) And it came to pass, as the camels had done drinking, that the man took a golden earring of half a shekel weight, and two bracelets for her hands of ten shekels weight of gold;

23) And said, Whose daughter art thou (you)? tell me, I pray thee (beg of you): is there room in thy (your) father's house for <u>us</u> (this is the first mention of others with the servant) to lodge in? (Now we know the trip up and back probably took a lot longer, no man or woman can walk or run as fast as a camel and keep it up for hours on end, ever day)

24) And she said unto him, I am the daughter of Bethuel (Bethuel is the father of Rebekah) the son of Milcah (Milcah is the mother of Bethuel and grandmother of Rebekah), which she bare unto Nahor (Nahor is the father of Bethuel and grandfather of Rebekah. Nahor and Abraham were brothers, both from their father Terah, and Isaac is Abraham's son. Isaac and Bethuel, the father of Rebekah, are first-cousins).

25) She said moreover unto him, We have both straw and provender (Dry food for domestic animals) (Merriam-Webster) enough, and room to lodge in (God had her go over and above what the servant asked God for to begin with. Going over and above what someone asks God for would

make someone nervous and start doubting if the sign really was from God in today's society. They ask God to bless them, then when He does, they wonder if the blessing really is from God to begin with because it's not exactly what they ask for to their specifications, but it is to God's specifications. Remember the servant only asked God to have the woman to draw water for him and the camels as well, nothing to do with food and provisions).

26) And the man bowed down his head, and worshipped the LORD.

27) And he (the servant) said, Blessed be the LORD God of my master Abraham, who hath not left destitute my master of his mercy and his truth: I being in the way, the LORD led me to the house of my master's brethren.

28) And the damsel ran, and told them of her mother's house (All the people in her mother's house including the servants) these things.

29) And Rebekah had a brother, and his name was Laban: and Laban ran out unto the man, unto the well.

30) And it came to pass, when he (Laban) saw the earring and bracelets upon his sister's hands, and when he heard the words of Rebekah his sister, saying, Thus spake the man unto me; that he came unto the man; and, behold, he stood by the camels at the well (Rebekah's brother didn't even ask for a confirmation, he took the word of Abraham's servant as Rebekah did. Now what woman today is going to do that without confirmation? Yet women keep praying for Jesus to send them a Christian man all the time and wonder why Jesus doesn't answer. Jesus does answer, they aren't listening. That makes me wonder how close the women are to Christ. They need confirmation, and then they want the confirmation to be from someone who isn't even praying to bring a future husband to them. That means they are doubting instead of walking in faith. How many confirmations did Noah have? None. Yet he spent months, maybe even years with a bright blue, hot, sunny sky over his head).

31) And he said, Come in, thou blessed of the LORD; wherefore standest thou without? for I have prepared the house, and room for the camels (The house is ready for the servant and there is room for the camels in what we would call a barn as well).

32) And the man came into the house: and he ungirded (What we would call taking backpacks and bridles off, the bridle is the mouth piece with the reigns attached if you didn't know) his camels, and gave straw and

provender (food) for the camels, and water to wash his (The servant Abraham sent) feet, and the **men's feet that were with him** (This is the first mention of several men being with the servant on the journey. I seriously doubt they walked that distance, they probably rode. This confirms the camel's loads were pretty close to maximum weight).

33) And there was set meat before him to eat: but he said, I will not eat, until I have told mine errand (The servant wouldn't take part in anything until his business was completed with the brother). And he (the brother) said, Speak on.

34) And he said, I am Abraham's servant.

35) And the LORD hath blessed my master greatly; and he is become great: and he hath given him flocks, and herds, and silver, and gold, and menservants, and maidservants, and camels, and asses.

36) And Sarah my master's wife bare a son to my master when she was old: and unto him hath he given all that he hath.

37) And my master made me swear, saying, Thou shalt not take a wife to my son of the daughters of the Canaanites, in whose land I dwell (Not to have Isaac to be 'unequally yoked'):

38) But thou shalt go unto my father's house, and to my kindred, and take a wife unto my son.

39) And I said unto my master, Peradventure (just in case) the woman will not follow me.

40) And he said unto me, The LORD, before whom I walk, will send his angel with thee, and prosper thy way; and thou shalt take a wife for my son of my kindred, and of my father's house:

41) Then shalt thou (you) be clear from this my oath, when thou comest to my kindred; and if they give not thee one, thou shalt be clear from my oath.

42) And I came this day unto the well, and said, O LORD God of my master Abraham, if now thou do prosper my way which I go:

43) Behold, I stand by the well of water; and it shall come to pass, that when the virgin cometh forth to draw water, and I say to her, Give me, I pray thee, a little water of thy pitcher to drink;

44) And she say to me, Both drink thou, and I will also draw for thy camels: let the same be the woman whom the LORD hath appointed out for my master's son.

45) And before I had done speaking **in mine heart**, behold, Rebekah came

forth with her pitcher on her shoulder; and she went down unto the well, and drew water: and I said unto her, Let me drink, I pray thee.

Isaiah 65:24

And it shall come to pass, that **before they call, I will answer**; and **while they are yet speaking, I will hear** (This reminds me of when I asked Jesus to go ahead and 'sanctify Detta through me' so Jesus could protect her when she was kidnapped and taken to Satan World Order Headquarters. He couldn't help her or protect her until I told Him to go ahead and sanctify her through me from my heart. That's in MATTHEW'S WORD 'TWO':REAL WORD OF GOD BIBLE).

46) And she (Rebekah) made haste, and let down her pitcher from her shoulder, and said, Drink, and I will give thy (your) camels drink also: so I drank, and she made the camels drink also.

47) And I asked her (Rebekah), and said, Whose daughter art thou? And she (Rebekah) said, the daughter of Bethuel, Nahor's son, whom Milcah bare unto him: and I put the earring upon her face, and the bracelets upon her hands.

48) And I bowed down my head, and worshipped the LORD, and blessed the LORD God of my master Abraham, which had led me in the right way to take my master's brother's daughter unto his son.

49) And now if ye will deal kindly and truly with my master, tell me: and if not, tell me; that I may turn to the right hand, or to the left (Abraham's servant wants to know if they will let Rebekah go with him to Isaac or not, so the servant will know what to do next).

50) Then Laban and Bethuel answered and said, The thing proceedeth from the LORD: we cannot speak unto thee bad or good (Laban and Bethuel won't go against what God wants to happen, they consent to Rebekah going to Isaac).

51) Behold, Rebekah is before thee (you), take her, and go, and let her (Rebekah) be thy (your) master's son's (Isaac's) wife, as the LORD hath spoken (Even now, no one asked for a confirmation from God).

52) And it came to pass, that, when Abraham's servant heard their words, he worshipped the LORD, bowing himself to the earth.

53) And the servant brought forth jewels of silver, and jewels of gold, and raiment, and gave them to Rebekah: he (the servant) gave also to her (Rebekah's) brother and to her (Rebekah's) mother precious things.

54) And they did eat and drink, he (Abraham's servant) and the men that

were with him, and tarried (stayed) all night; and they rose up in the morning, and he (Abraham's servant) said, Send me away unto my master (The servant asking to be excused with Rebekah).

55) And her (Rebekah's) brother and her (Rebekah's) mother said, Let the damsel abide with us a few days, at the least ten; after that she (Rebekah) shall go (Wanting to keep the men around for a few days, possibly to receive more pay for their stay).

56) And he (Abraham's servant) said unto them (Rebekah's mother and brother), Hinder me not (Don't hold me back), seeing the LORD hath prospered my way; send me away that I may go to my master.

57) And they (Rebekah's mother and brother) said, We will call the damsel, and enquire at her mouth (Actually asking Rebekah what she wished to do. Rebekah's Free Will).

58) And they called Rebekah, and said unto her, Wilt thou go with this man? And she said, I will go (With her own Free Will, Rebekah chose to go that very day by herself. Rebekah knew she had a new family and new responsibilities to her new family. Rebekah was looking out for the well-being of her new family instead of her old family. Rebekah also knew if she stayed there, it would cost her and her new family more precious goods. Another point that needs to be made here is that Rebekah knows nothing at all about Isaac. Just like Isaac knows nothing at all about Rebekah, except they were from the same 'Proper Physical Bloodline'. Rebekah is going totally by faith to her future husband at the word of a servant of her future husband's father, not even the servant of her future husband. How many women today would do that even though they keep praying for God to send them Christian men?).

59) And they sent away Rebekah their sister, and her (Rebekah's) nurse, and Abraham's servant, and his men (Now we have more people who are going to be riding on a camel on the journey back to Canaan).

60) And they blessed Rebekah, and said unto her, Thou art our sister, be thou the mother of thousands of millions, and let thy seed possess the gate of those which hate them.

61) And Rebekah arose, and her damsels (Now Rebekah has damsels going with her and not just her nurse), and they rode upon the camels (Some had to walk on their journey back. That slowed them down even more), and followed the man: and the servant took Rebekah, and went his way (now they had at least three weeks of traveling by camel on the

journey back home. We also need to remember that now all of Rebekah's damsels were with her and some of the damsels from Rebekah and servants of Abraham had to have been walking all that distance. That trip back was longer than the trip to Rebekah. Why? They started out in Hebron as was going to Kadesh-Barnea where Isaac lived. For estimation purposes we can use the same numbers from Hebron to Ur, but reverse them, then we will need to add on some more mileage from Hebron to Kadesh-Barnea. From Ur to Mari is about 400 miles or 668 kilometers west, from Mari to Damascus is about 300 miles or 501 kilometers south west, and from Damascus to Hebron is about 160 miles or 167.2 kilometers south. From Ur to is Hebron 160+300+400=860 miles or 167.2+501+668=1,336.2 kilometers south west. Now we need to add from Hebron to Kadesh-Barnea where Isaac was living at that time is about 75 miles or 125.25 kilometers south. So let's add that on to the 860 miles we already have. 860 miles+75 miles=935 miles from Ur to Kadesh-Barnea/25 miles per day=37.4 days/6 =6.2 weeks. Remember, 1.67 kilometer=1 mile (Merriam-Webster). The Round Trip from Hebron to Ur was 860 miles or 1,336.2 kilometers and 860 miles or 1,336.2 from Ur to Hebron + Hebron to Kadesh-Barnea is 75 miles or 125.5 kilometers=860+860+75=1,795 miles or 1.67x1795=2,997.65 kilometers. 1,795miles/25 miles per day=71.8 days/6=11.9 or 12 weeks round trip. They couldn't travel that fast with people walking now instead of everyone riding camels. My point with all these facts about the camels and all the time involved in the journey is this. What do you think Rebekah was talking to the servants about during that period of time? They could have counted each and every rock or every sand dune and possibly any bugs or animals in the desert. No, Rebekah was asking the servants about Isaac, Abraham, and Sarah the whole time. This is also when the servants told Rebekah about Hagar and Ishmael and what happened to them. By the time Rebekah arrived at her new home and saw Isaac for the first time, she knew everything about him, Isaac's likes, dislikes, favorite foods, favorite past-time, favorite color, favorite clothes, how he would act and re-act in different situations, what pleased him, what made him angry, etc, Rebekah knew Isaac like the back of her hand. She could have told anyone how long it took for Isaac to have breakfast, how to fix his bath water, anything about Isaac, Rebekah knew everything about Isaac before she ever arrived to see him in person and Isaac knew nothing about Rebekah, except she was the wife that God picked out for him.   Rebekah knew nothing about Isaac before she left her brother's house and Isaac knew nothing about Rebekah before he married her. The only thing Rebekah knew is that God had set it up and that was out of the mouth of Abraham's servant, not Abraham, not Isaac, but Abraham's servant who asked God for one particular sign about which woman to take back to Isaac, Isaac didn't even know that much.   God chose what Abraham requested, a wife from his own family bloodline to keep the 'Proper Physical Bloodline Clean'. If you don't know anything about the 'Proper Physical Bloodline', then you need to purchase my book called 'MATTHEW'S WORD 'TWO':REAL WORD OF GOD BIBLE and read it, there is a whole section about the Spiritual Bloodline and Physical Bloodline. All this happened without even one confirmation).

62) And Isaac came from the way of <u>the well Lahairoi; for he dwelt in the</u> **<u>south country,</u>** (in Canaan).

63) And Isaac went out to meditate (pray) in the field at the eventide (noon): and he lifted up his eyes, and saw, and, behold, the camels were coming.

64) And Rebekah lifted up her eyes, and when she saw Isaac, she lighted off the camel.

65) For she had said unto the servant, What man is this that walketh in the field to meet us? And the servant had said, It is my master: therefore she took a vail, and covered herself (As soon as she knew the man in the field was Isaac, she covered her face with a vail and jumped off the camel).

66) And the servant told Isaac all things that he had done.

67) And Isaac brought her (Rebekah) into his mother Sarah's tent (<u>Sarah was in the **south country** with Isaac, in Canaan</u>) and took (laid with, made love to) Rebekah, and she became his wife (Nothing else was required to have a marriage); and he loved her: and Isaac was comforted (by Rebekah) after his mother's death. (Sarah, Isaac's mother had been dead for three years now)

Genesis 25:20-34

20) And Isaac was forty years old when he took Rebekah to wife, the daughter of Bethuel the Syrian of Padanaram, the sister to Laban the Syrian.

21) And Isaac intreated (variation of entreat: to plead with especially in

order to persuade: ask urgently) (Merriam-Webster) the LORD for his wife, because she (Rebekah) was barren (couldn't conceive. Sounds like Sarai when she was barren): and the LORD was intreated (Variation of entreat: to plead with especially in order to persuade: ask urgently) (Merriam-Webster) of him, and Rebekah his wife conceived.

22) And the children struggled together within her; and she said, If it be so, why am I thus? And she went to enquire (ask) of the LORD.

23) And the LORD said unto her, Two nations are in thy womb, and two manner of people shall be separated from thy bowels (interior parts) (Merriam-Webster); and the one people shall be stronger than the other people; and the elder shall serve the younger (the future being foretold).

24) And when her days to be delivered were fulfilled (she gave birth), behold, there were twins in her womb.

25) And the first came out red, all over like an hairy garment; and they called his name Esau.

26) And after that came his brother out, and his hand took hold on Esau's heel (The two brothers are already fighting between each other); and his name was called Jacob: and Isaac was threescore years old (sixty) when she (Rebekah) bare them.

27) And the boys grew: and Esau was a cunning hunter, a man of the field; and Jacob was a plain man, dwelling in tents.

28) And Isaac loved Esau, because he did eat of his venison: but Rebekah loved Jacob (This is not good, each parent having a favorite child. Each child should be loved equally by both parent).

29) And Jacob sod pottage (Made vegetable beef soup): and Esau came from the field, and he was faint:

30) And Esau said to Jacob, Feed me, I pray thee, with that same red pottage; for I am faint: therefore was his name called Edom (Esau's name is changed to Edom).

31) And Jacob said, Sell me this day thy birthright (Their offspring are still fighting each other to this very day).

32) And Esau said, Behold, I am at the point to die: and what profit shall this birthright do to me? (Sounds like Christians selling their Heavenly Birthright by denying Christ in public and private meetings so they can receive Government Assistance of one type or another)

33) And Jacob said, Swear to me this day; and he (Esau) sware unto him (Jacob): and he (Esau) sold his birthright unto Jacob (I've actually had to

use this scripture filling out United States and county government grievance forms complaining that governmental agencies wanted me to deny Christ to take part in government programs. Of course I refused to deny Christ, but I wasn't allowed to participate in the government programs either. The governmental agency wanted me to sell my Heavenly Birthright for their help in their governmental program. Denying Christ is selling your Heavenly Birthright. We deny Christ in front of man, Christ will deny us in front of the Angels in Heaven and the Father in Heaven. More about this subject in my book called, 'WHAT'S WRONG WITH THIS PICTURE?' that will be out within the next year. I have to learn how to use some more programs on this computer in order to write that book. There will be a lot of legal papers and a picture of me covered in my own blood after I was beaten by an old girlfriend on the cover).

34) Then Jacob gave Esau bread and pottage (soup) of lentiles (Edible plants, vegetable beef soup); and he (Esau) did eat and drink, and rose up, and went his way: thus Esau despised his birthright (If I would have accepted the governmental agencies proposal to leave Jesus outside the meetings then I would have sold my birthright for the same bowl of pottage).

Genesis 26:1-35
1) And there was a famine in the land, beside the first famine that was in the days of Abraham. And Isaac went unto Abimelech king of the Philistines unto Gerar. (Kadesh-Barnea to Gerar is about 55 miles or 91.85 kilometers north-west/25 miles a day=2.2 days)
2) And the LORD appeared unto him, and said, Go not down into Egypt; dwell in the land which I shall tell thee of:
3) Sojourn in this land (Gerar), and I will be with thee, (Here is another stipulation of God being with us and blessing us. We do as He says and He is with us and bless us, we don't do as He says and we are on our own because He can't protect us any longer, that's our free-will) and will bless thee; for unto thee, and unto thy seed, I will give all these countries, and I will perform the oath which I sware unto Abraham thy father (Here again God says it's because of Abraham, the prophet, that all this is done for Isaac. Isaac and Ishmael were never Prophets, Abraham was);
4) And I will make thy (your) seed (offspring) to multiply as the stars of

heaven, and will give unto thy seed (your offspring) all these countries; and in thy seed (your offspring) shall all the nations of the earth be blessed;

5) Because that Abraham obeyed my voice, and kept my charge, my commandments, my statutes, and my laws. (A lot of Christians don't keep his commandments or statutes, or laws anymore, then they wonder why Christ doesn't bless them. That's why, because they don't do as He commands)

6) And **Isaac dwelt in Gerar**:

7) And the men of the place asked him (Isaac) of his wife (Rebekah); and he (Isaac) said, She is my sister: for he feared to say, She is my wife; lest, said he, the men of the place should kill me for Rebekah; because she was fair to look upon (Isaac lied just like his dad, Abram).

8) And it came to pass, when he had been there a long time, that Abimelech king of the Philistines looked out at a window, and saw, and, behold, Isaac was sporting (flirting, passionately kissing on her, possibly touching her as a husband would and not a brother would) with Rebekah his wife.

9) And Abimelech called Isaac, and said, Behold, **of a surety she is thy wife** (Yep, Abraham was definitely **showing** Rebekah was his wife and not his sister); and how saidst thou, She is my sister? And Isaac said unto him, Because I said, Lest I die for her.

10) And Abimelech said, What is this thou hast done unto us? one of the people might lightly have lien with thy wife, and thou shouldest have brought guiltiness upon us (**Laying with someone's husband or wife is a very wicked thing to do and curses fall upon those who do it. Those curses are still active today**).

11) And Abimelech charged all his people, saying, **He that toucheth this man or his wife shall surely be put to death** (The penalty of Adultery is DEATH. Adultery is not to be taken lightly).

12) Then Isaac sowed (Put forth the effort) in that land, and **received** (Hey, everyone, this is after all the business expenses and taxes are taken out) **in the same year an hundredfold: and the LORD blessed him**.

13) And the man (Isaac) waxed (Easily changed) great, and went forward, and grew (In God) until he became very great (Isaac was willing to be changed by God and molded into what God wanted him to become):

14) For he had possession of flocks, and possession of herds, and great

store of servants: and the Philistines envied him.

15) For all the wells which his father's servants had digged in the days of Abraham his father, the Philistines had stopped them, and filled them with earth (Sounds like the Philistines were jealous of Isaac and Abraham too).

16) And Abimelech said unto Isaac, Go from us; for thou art much mightier than we.

17) And Isaac departed thence, and pitched his tent in the valley of Gerar, and dwelt there. (Gerar and the valley of Gerar are two different places, but close to each other. In Verse 6 Isaac and Rebekah were in Gerar, now they are in the valley of Gerar)

18) And Isaac digged again the wells of water, which they had digged in the days of Abraham his father; for the Philistines had stopped them after the death of Abraham: and he called their names after the names by which his father had called them (Digging wells that were already there at one time. There must have been some kind of markers or something to pin-point the wells).

19) And Isaac's servants digged in the valley, and found there a well of springing water.

20) And the herdmen of Gerar (See, Gerar and the valley of Gerar are very close to each other) did strive with Isaac's herdmen, saying, The water is ours: and he called the name of the well Esek; because they strove (fought) with him.

21) And they digged another well, and strove (fought) for that also: and he called the name of it Sitnah.

22) And he removed from thence, and digged another well; and for that they strove not (Didn't fight this time. It took three times to settle down, moved twice): and he called the name of it Rehoboth; and he said, For now the LORD hath made room for us, and we shall be fruitful in the land.

23) And **he (Isaac) went up from thence (there) to Beersheba**. (From Gerar to Beersheba is about 20 miles or 33.4 kilometers south-east/25 miles per day=0.8 of a day)

24) And the LORD appeared unto him (Isaac) the same night, and said, I am the God of Abraham thy father: fear not, for I am with thee, and **will bless thee, and multiply thy seed for my servant Abraham's sake** (Again, this proves Isaac and Ishmael were never prophets, God is keeping His promise to Abraham, not to Isaac or Ishmael. If anyone is wondering why I keep bringing up the fact that Isaac or Ishmael were never prophets,

it's because from what I understand, Islam is founded on the prophet Ishmael and Muslim is a branch off Islam, so if there was never a prophet Ishmael to begin with, then there can not be a Heavenly religion of Islam or Muslim, they both stem from a 'Religious Unclean Spirit' that made Ishmael a 'wild man' to begin with, remember Ishmael married an 'Idol Worshipper', from Egypt and dwelt as a 'wild man' in the Wilderness of Paran. Just like the man who came to Jesus with the 'Legion' in him was a 'wild man', remember? Jesus commanded the 'Legion' into the swine?).
25) And he builded an altar there, and called upon the name of the LORD, and pitched his tent there: and there Isaac's servants digged a well.
26) Then Abimelech went to him from Gerar, and Ahuzzath one of his friends, and Phichol the chief captain of his army.
27) And Isaac said unto them, Wherefore come ye to me, seeing ye hate me, and have sent me away from you?
28) And they said, We saw certainly that the LORD was with thee: and we said, Let there be now an oath betwixt (between) us, even betwixt (between) us and thee (you), and let us make a covenant with thee (you); (Now Abimelech wants to kiss and make up seeing is proof that God is with Isaac, everyone wants a blessing. Talk about the same thing happening today. No one wants anything to do with you until they see with their own eyes that Jesus Christ of Nazareth is on your side, then everyone wants a part of it. Having peace is one thing, being a part of the 'blessings from Jesus' must be learned and lived on an individual basis).
29) That thou wilt do us no hurt, as we have not touched thee, and as we have done unto thee nothing but good (This leaves a lot of room, nothing but good? What about the times Isaac had to re-dig all the wells that Abraham dug in the beginning and they were still kicked out after Abimelech gave them permission to stay on his land. Sounds like they want that kind of good to be done to them), and have sent thee away in peace (Isaac did sent them away in peace, but that's all they got): thou art now the blessed of the LORD.
30) And he made them a feast, and they did eat and drink.
31) And they rose up betimes in the morning, and sware one to another: and Isaac sent them away, and they departed from him in peace.
32) And it came to pass the same day, that Isaac's servants came, and told him concerning the well which they had digged, and said unto him, We have found water.

33) And <u>he (Isaac) called it Shebah</u>:   therefore the name of the city is <u>Beersheba</u> unto this day.

34) And Esau was forty years old when he took to wife Judith the daughter of Beeri the Hittite (The same tribe who Abraham went to for Sarah's burial place), and Bashemath the daughter of Elon the Hittite (Esau was still angry and became 'unequally yoked' with a woman outside the 'Proper Physical Bloodline', that make her outside the 'Proper Spiritual Bloodline' as well. That's why it was a 'grief of mind' to Isaac and Rebekah):   (Esau married out of the 'Proper Physical Bloodline' before Jacob and Rebekah tricked Isaac for Isaac to bless Jacob instead of Esau even though Esau is the oldest son)

35) Which were a grief of mind unto Isaac and to Rebekah. (Esau and Judith are 'Unequally Yoked', they don't fit well together in the marriage bond to each other)

(CONTINUED IN:
HEAVENLY ANGEL LAY LAY
EXPLAINS WHY PROFESSIONAL COUNSELORS
HAVE 'HARDENED HEARTS')

BIBLIOGRAPHY

1. Merriam Webster's Collegiate Dictionary Tenth Edition (1993), United States of America.

2. The Holy Bible King James Version (1998), B. B. Kirkbride Bible Co., Inc. Indianapolis, IN..USA